5 STEPS TO RAISING CONFIDENT KIDS: How to Raise Smart, Confident Kids and Prepare them for Success

Edward George

Table of contents

Chapter 1

25 Things You Can Do Right Now To Build a Child's Confidence

Certainty is crucially critical to a kid's future bliss, wellbeing, and achievement. Sure youngsters are better outfitted to manage peer pressure, obligation, disappointments, challenges, and both positive and pessimistic feelings.
Furthermore, what is the KEY calculate fostering a youngster's certainty?

YOU! The kid's folks and educators.

No tension, correct? Simply sit back and relax - building a kid's certainty doesn't need to be a scary or muddled task.

You can make it fun!

Utilize these 25 exploration-based, powerful procedures to begin helping the certainty of your kids or understudies today.

1. Guarantee they realize your affection is unrestricted.
How we see our children (or how our children accept we see them) significantly affects how they see themselves.

Make it clear to your kids (or to your understudies) that you love and care for them in any event, when they go with errors or unfortunate choices, and try not to cruelly reprimand or disgrace them.

2. Practice positive self-talk with them.
The two kids and grown-ups frequently participate in negative and harming gab with themselves: "I can't do this," or, "I'm awful at ___________," or, "What's up with me?"

Model and show kids positive assertions utilizing our famous and free Affirmation Bracelets action.

3. Address them by their name.
Tending to youngsters by name is a strong and straightforward method for sending the message that they're significant, particularly when matched with a well-disposed eye-to-eye connection.

4. Give them age-proper "exceptional assignments" to take care of you.
Notwithstanding errands and study hall occupations, give kids "extraordinary assignments" to assist them with feeling valuable, capable, and able. Utilizing "exceptional" gives youngsters much greater certainty and support.

In the home, these exceptional undertakings can incorporate assisting with a pet or more youthful kin depending on the situation, being your cooking "collaborator," or, for an extremely small kid, just dressing himself.

In the homeroom, children can assist with making study hall improvements, water plants, eradicating the board, and so forth.

5. Join their play (and let them lead). Participating in an easy breezy sends the message that he is significant and deserving of your time.

During recess, guardians can permit youngsters to start or pick the movement, as well as lead it. At the point when guardians take part in and seem to partake in a kid drove the movement, the kid feels significant and achieved.

Educators of small kids can execute this methodology in the study hall also.

6. Center around working on your certainty.

This isn't a stage you can achieve, for the time being, however, it's one of the most fundamental on this rundown.

Guardians are a kid's first and best good examples, so set aside some margin to fix your certainty if necessary. Begin by offering positive remarks about yourself as well as other people in your youngster's presence.

Educators, as well, ought to stay away from self-analysis and model trust before their understudies.

7. Ask them for their recommendation or assessment.
Ask kids for their recommendations or conclusions on age-proper circumstances to show that you esteem them and their thoughts.

This additionally assists youngsters with building certainty by exhibiting that even grown-ups need assistance at times, and it's OK to request it.

8. Make extraordinary time together.
Love and acknowledgment are key parts of certainty and self-esteem, so guardians ought to invest quality energy with their kids to exhibit that they are significant.

Take him on excursions, have supper together, mess around, head outside, or do whatever other movement permits you and your kid to partake in time together.

Educators can assist kids with feeling cherished and acknowledged by getting to know understudies' inclinations or leisure activities and trying out having customized discussions with every kid, similar to, "How was your soccer match yesterday, Sarah?" or, "I figure you could like this book about dinosaurs, Timmy."

9. Show them how to define and accomplish objectives.

Setting and accomplishing testing, reasonable objectives can assist kids with feeling more fit. Help your kids or understudies put forth and stick to explicit objectives by following the straightforward strides in our accommodating objective setting blog entry here.

10. Put away opportunities when you focus on them.

Guardians, your kid perceives when your psyche is on something different or when you're not genuinely focusing on him.

To assist your youngster with feeling esteemed and certain, put away the opportunity to take care of the hardware, reset your head, and genuinely concentrate on your kid.

Instructors, as well, can get some margin to offer understudies their full consideration and be mindful of their requirements.

11. Urge them to attempt a performance center class.

Theater classes are an extraordinary method for supporting certainty. Having a go at something new assists youngsters with feeling competent, and theater helps them to talk unhesitatingly before others and extend their usual range of familiarity.

Guardians and educators the same can urge children to evaluate a theater, and instructors might try and have the option to integrate pretending or show games into the homeroom.

12. Acclaim them the correct way.

Essentially giving youngsters acclaim isn't successful, however, commending kids the correct way can assemble their confidence.

Give youngsters veritable, explicit commendation that centers more around exertion than on results (like getting straight A's) or on fixed capacities (like knowledge).

13. Free Your Words
Allow them to hear you talking emphatically about them to other people.
Another fast, simple method for supporting a kid's certainty is to "incidentally" let him hear you commending his incredible accomplishments and endeavors to other people.

Kids are now and again suspicious when we straightforwardly acclaim them, however hearing you rehash this commendation to others makes it more trustworthy (and, surprisingly, more significant).

14. Oppose contrasting them with others.
Try not to contrast kids with kin or colleagues with questions like, "For what reason might you at any point act like

him/her?" or, "Look how well your sister does in school! For what reason mightn't you at any point do that?"

These examinations make kids question themselves, accept that they can't satisfy you or measure up to your assumptions, and at last lose certainty.

15. Give age-suitable undertakings around the house or homeroom.
At the point when children take care of errands or little positions, they feel that they are making an important commitment, which provides them with a feeling of skill and certainty.

Give your youngster age-proper obligations like making the bed, taking care of the canine, preparing the table, collapsing garments, getting toys, and so forth.

Relegate your understudies' assignments like taking care of provisions or passing out papers.

16. Develop their feeling of having a place by hanging their pictures or craftsmanship around the home or study hall.
Indeed, even something as straightforward as hanging family pictures around your home can expand your youngster's certainty!

In the homeroom, as well, you can post photos of your understudies. You can likewise have them make self-pictures, plan banners or interconnecting pieces that address their characters and interests, and so forth and, hang these around the homeroom.

This provides kids with a feeling of having a place, acknowledgment, and love that will, at last, assist their certainty with taking off.

17. Allow them to settle on age-suitable decisions.
Like errands and unique assignments, decisions assist youngsters with feeling skillful and strong.

Permit youngsters to pursue age-fitting choices like what to wear, what to have for breakfast, what game to play or variety to utilize, where to go on an excursion, and so on.

Educators can incorporate decisions into the homeroom by allowing understudies to come to conclusions about how they will exhibit the dominance of expertise (show what they realize about weather conditions by drawing an image, composing a melody, or making a story) or by allowing the class to examine and pick specific books or exercises.

18. Urge them to attempt new things to foster new abilities.

Youngsters who need certainty frequently avoid attempting new things or handling new difficulties. Pay attention to this episode of the Big Life Kids digital broadcast with your kid to urge them to take a stab at a genuinely new thing!

Support the kids in your day-to-day existence to fan out, attempt new exercises, and foster new abilities. This gives kids the certainty that they can handle anything that comes in their direction.

19. Assist them with finding their inclinations and interests.
Children should find their inclinations and interests. At the point when kids find what they like and succeed at, they gain trust in themselves and their capacities.

Set out open doors for your kids or understudies to attempt exercises that interest them, and be steady in these undertakings.

20. Assist them with defeating the feeling of dread toward disappointment.
The anxiety toward disappointment frequently keeps kids from making an honest effort and arriving at their fullest potential, which can normally decrease certainty.

Assist jokes with beating the feeling of dread toward disappointment by instructing them that mix-ups are a satisfactory piece of life and that individuals seldom make progress without difficulties and misfortunes.

21. Urge them to communicate their sentiments.
At the point when you condemn or neglect a kid's sentiments, he might feel that his feelings don't make any difference and infer that this implies he doesn't make any difference by the same token.

Urge youngsters to communicate both positive and gloomy feelings, and assist them with solidly talking through these feelings.

22. Ensure they realize you're annoyed with their decisions, not with what their identity is.
Flying off the handle with your kids or understudies some of the time is inescapable, and you should offer valuable analysis and outcomes.

Nonetheless, clarify the kid's decisions or activities you're angry with, not who the youngster is personally. Direct all analysis at these activities as opposed to censuring the kid with articulations like, "That is no joke!" or, "For what reason would you say you are so messy?"

23. Encompass them with positive, certain individuals (counting their companions).

The more a kid is around certain, sure people, the likelier he is to turn into a certain and positive individual himself.

Guardians, give your youngster solid grown-up good examples and give your all to guarantee that his companions are certain individuals who elevate and support your kid instead of destroying him.

Instructors, be positive and sure good examples for your understudies and help your understudies to be thoughtful and construct each other up.

24. Make a Wall of Fame perceive their accomplishments.

In the home or the study hall, you can exhibit your pride and appreciation for youngsters' accomplishments by making a "Mass of Fame" that features accomplishments like passing marks, workmanship undertakings, prizes or testaments, and photos of the kid taking part in sports or other most loved exercises, from there, the sky is the limit.

A Wall of Fame can feature a youngster's work and assurance, giving him certainty and support that can be particularly useful amid self-question.

25. Give them embraces!
Actual fondness imparts love, acknowledgment, and having a place, making kids blissful and certain.

Guardians and instructors of more youthful youngsters can give kids high fives, back taps, hair dishevels, and bunches of embraces to show that they are focused on and esteemed

Chapter 2

Close to home Validation: How to Validate a Child's Feelings (33 Examples)

| What is close to home approval | Why is it significant | How to approve in 3 stages | 33 models |

Kids in certain societies are shown they ought to be seen-and-not-heard. This infers "you don't make any difference".

What a terrible inclination that is.

We all need to feel that we matter. We need to be heard and acknowledged.

Approving a kid's sentiments doesn't mean you concur with them. It implies telling a youngster that they are heard and perceived.

When done accurately, the effect of approval on a kid's improvement is huge.

What Is Emotional Validation

Profound approval is the demonstration of tuning in, recognizing, and tolerating someone else's sentiments, regardless of whether they're negative. It includes standing by listening to others express their feelings without disregarding, excusing, deprecating, dismissing, or passing judgment on them regardless of whether you concur with their profound reaction.

Approving a kid includes guaranteeing them that their sentiments, contemplations, and inside experiences are substantial

It is one of the most important nurturing and relationship abilities.

Why Is Emotional Validation Important

Profound approval is significant to a kid's turn of events.

During youth, guardians who approve structure a close-to-home association with their youngsters. At the point when youngsters are permitted to communicate areas of strength for them, they foster a feeling that all is well with the world. They feel open to being transparent with their connection figure. They additionally figure out how to foster self-empathy which is related to secure connection

Profound REGULATION

Approved kids figure out how to grasp their close-to-home encounters and direct their sentiments with the assistance of their folks.

Feeling excusal, then again, may add to challenges in feeding guideline

Emotional wellness

Youngsters who get profound approval experience a lift in self-esteem. They foster a sound feeling of character and will generally have better emotional wellness.

Profound refutation in youth might prompt the improvement of a psychological wellness condition, for example, marginal behavioral condition (BPD) or posttraumatic stress jumble (PTSD)

How Do You Emotionally Validate A Child

Approval can be utilized with a kid who is showing pessimistic feelings.

Notwithstanding, powerful approval can be precarious to do. At the point when guardians approve, they should accept care not to fall into old propensities.

Here are the three moves toward approving a kid's gloomy sentiments.

Stage 1 - NOTICE

Try not to disregard or imagine you don't see it when a kid is vexed. Rather, affirm that you notice their pessimistic feelings.

"I saw you fall when you attempted to get up to speed with me."

"I heard that you just lost the game."

"Your sister disregarded you when you attempted to converse with her."

Stage 2 - ACKNOWLEDGE

Recognize what the kid is feeling inside and distinguish where it comes from.

Assuming the youngster can talk, utilize empathic tuning in (or undivided attention) to listen to them. If the kid is excessively youthful or excessively agitated, train them to name their sentiments.

"You should be extremely vexed because I didn't sit tight for you."

"That feels extremely uncalled for because you played so well in the game."

"It feels so destructive. It's as if she couldn't have cared less about you."

Stage 3 - WITNESS

Here is the vital step where many guardians commit an error.

While many guardians get the idea of approval, they might in any case neglect to quiet an agitated kid since they don't follow this step.

It is right now many guardians will attempt to make sense of why the kid shouldn't feel as such or offer spontaneous guidance. There is a certain feeling of nullification here that the kid had some unacceptable inclination. This fixes everything in stages 1 and 2, exacerbating things.

As of now, you truly don't have to say anything more. Stay with the youngster and express sympathy and attunement with your look or non-verbal communication.

To help them to "think unexpectedly" or understand things according to an improved point of view, do it later. This present time isn't the ideal open door for that kind of reaction.

This is a period for your youngster to grasp their sentiments, acknowledge them, and structure a feeling guideline procedure, not a period for addresses.

Examples Of Validating Statements

I can see the reason why you are vexed.

That should be hard.

That's just terrible!

That should baffle

That is so miserable.

What a yucky day for you!

Let me know what occurred.

It's a good idea that you feel upset.

It is a seriously big deal to you.

I realize it should truly sting. Do you need an embrace?

I would feel awful in that situation, as well.

What something horrendous they said!

You needed to help however didn't understand they didn't need it.

I'd have that impression, as well.

What you're feeling is ordinary.

Your sentiments are substantial.

There are no off-base sentiments.

You needn't bother with their authorization to feel.

Please accept my apologies that I hurt you.

Having that impression is typical.

That was a major fall. I'm so happy you're alright.

Much thanks to you for discussing your thoughts with me.

Please accept my apologies.

It's a good idea that you feel went after.

I concur that was off-base of them.

I can't accept that they did that by the same token.

That feels so off-base. I'm happy you stayed with your choice.

You were so courageous.

You persisted.

I saw you were exceptionally quiet notwithstanding all the tumult.

It is alright to cry. Try not to regret it.

Feeling as such is on the right track.

Oof, that appears as though it harms.

Profound approval is remembering another person's sentiments or necessities without judgment. You don't need to concur with somebody's viewpoint to approve of their feelings. You simply need to show the individual that you comprehend how they could feel how they do.

For what reason is it vital to approve your youngster's feelings?
At the point when you approve of your kid's feelings, you can:

Assist your youngster with feeling seen, comprehended, and esteemed.
Assist your kid with figuring out how to distinguish their feelings and work through them.

Show your kid that you're somebody they can entrust with their sentiments.

Help your youngster to be more tolerant of gloomy sentiments. This can assist them with keeping mentally collected and handling those sentiments when they occur.

Approving your youngster's feelings can likewise assist your kid with learning self-sympathy. At the point when individuals have self-sympathy, they are bound to have the option to manage difficulty and mishaps solidly.

Approving your youngster's feelings

It's critical to show your kid that you comprehend how they're feeling and that you're willing to tune in. Here are a few things you can do to approve your kid's feelings.

Truly tune in.

Show your kid that you're keen on the thing they're feeling and why. How it's done:

Center just around your youngster, without interruption.Show that you're tuning in by utilizing your non-verbal communication and voice.

You can sit at eye level with your kid, incline in toward them, and gesture your head as they talk. You can make statements like "Mmmhmmm," and, "Gracious, I understand."

Let your kid know that you comprehend what they're feeling and why. You can make statements like, "I see. You blew up when your sibling tore your drawing. That should be so baffling since you buckled down on it."

Recollect that your kid's concerns are as genuine to them as yours are to you.
Something that appears little to you may be an extremely huge thing to your kid.

For instance, finding a place with a group could appear to mean quite a bit to you now as a grown-up. Be that as it may, for your kid, being viewed as "various" or not fitting in may feel like a major issue.

Be certifiable.
Children can frequently tell when grown-ups intend what they say, versus when they're trying to say the "right words." You may not truly comprehend the reason

why a lost pullover merits a gigantic implosion.

However, you likely comprehend the dissatisfaction of losing something essential to you. Center around that.

Allow your youngster to feel the feeling completely.
Telling somebody to "quit stressing" or to "unwind" when they're vexed typically doesn't function admirably.

Furthermore, telling your kid not to feel a specific way is like saying, "What you're feeling is off-base or not satisfactory." It doesn't assist your kid with figuring out how to perceive and manage troublesome feelings. All things being equal, it trains them to keep away from and smother those sentiments. Attempt this:

Rather than saying: "Don't be senseless. You can't stand Eli! He's your dearest companion!"
You can say: "Goodness. You should be truly distraught at Eli. I bet it's difficult to feel so furious with somebody you play with each day."

Do whatever it takes not to "fix" the issue to make the inclination disappear.
Assist your kid with figuring out how to recognize and manage sentiments and issues all alone. It's not difficult to need to safeguard your kid from having troublesome sentiments.

In any case, these sentiments are a piece of life. At the point when you don't attempt to save your kid from them, you are assisting your kid with mastering abilities for taking care of them.

Recall that each feeling is satisfactory, yet every way of behaving isn't.

Approving your kid's sentiments doesn't mean you need to give in each time your kid needs something. It likewise doesn't mean permitting your kid to act in unseemly ways.

For instance, it's useful to show understanding of your kid's displeasure at a jungle gym buddy. It's not approved to allow your youngster to communicate their displeasure by pushing the companion or expressing mean things.

Chapter 3

Fabricate areas of strength for your teen in the critical years

Fabricate serious areas of strength for your teen in the urgent years

Teens experience a flood of hormonal changes and there might be different conduct changes like peevishness, outrage, distress, lethargy, and need for seclusion on occasion.

As the brain research and physiology of a youngster begins transforming, they might encounter issues like pressure and close-to-home choppiness. It is vital to fix the establishment as this is the point at which the psyche is being modified and conviction frameworks are created.

Here are a few hints for guardians to deal with this stage better:

Empathy

Teens experience a flood of hormonal changes and there might be different social changes like peevishness, outrage, distress, lethargy, and need for detachment on occasion. This calls for guardians to be adoring, figuring out, mindful and strong yet it is additionally essential to know when to give them space. This assists the young person with fostering a feeling of solace and trust.

Self-assured correspondence

As your teen shows these progressions it tends to be perfect to have a discussion with them about what's in store in this period of life, the privileges and wrongs, how to oversee pressure, how you figure out them and are accessible to help them with any issues that they are managing.

Additionally, it is critical to have a conversation with them about worries like friend tensions, harassment, or any type of misuse and cause them to have a solid sense of reassurance and congenial to answer to you if there should be an occurrence of any such episode.

Such episodes can lastingly affect the brain research of the young person and on the off chance that managed perfectly can assist them with having a safer outlook on life.

Positive climate

At the point when teens see all their little and huge difficulties as dangers, it is fundamental to keep a good climate at home where they have a solid sense of reassurance seeing their folks cheerful, appreciation being rehearsed, positive words and language being utilized around them.

As kids advance more from perception than what is suspected of them, this helps an extraordinary arrangement in molding a positive conviction framework.

Profound breathing and active work

Teaching an act of taking eight to 10 full breaths five times each day, showing them straightforward contemplation procedures, and including actual work.

For example, cycling, swimming, yoga, or even a dance class can be extraordinary ways of delivering pressure and channelizing their energy as this assistance in delivering positive chemicals like serotonin and endorphins. This can give as a deep-rooted instrument to them to oversee pressure.

Confidence and assertions

Because of changes in chemicals, there are likewise different changes in the presence of a young person that begins to shake their certainty.

Causing a youngster to feel cherished and fostering the act of confidence and doing straightforward good confirmations, for example, 'I'm cherished, protected and upheld', 'I love and acknowledge myself, 'I'm an achiever, 'Life functions admirably for me, and so on, can be a splendid device to program their psyche mind decidedly.

Giving a teen the right direction, love and security can be the best gift a parent can give them throughout everyday life.

Giving solid groundwork is not exactly simple or easy. Following a debilitating day at work, it's more straightforward to gaze at the TV than audit your youngster's schoolwork; when your child accomplishes something wrong, it's simpler to allow it to slide than to be the "trouble maker" and discipline that person.

When your child is encircled by terrible impacts, it's more straightforward to take no notice, than to go up against the issue head-on; and when your kid meets rout, it's simpler to "fault the world" as opposed to assist your kid with tolerating liability and gain from the difficulty.

Step-by-step instructions to Build a Strong Foundation

Furnishing your children with solid groundwork is basic. The following are eight methods for building areas of strength for your children.

Sustaining. Nurturing is certainly not temporary work. Kids require consistent consolation and backing. Guardians are the team promoters who give trust and positive thinking to what's in store.

A disregard for one's own needs. Guardians are magnanimous individuals ready to swear off an incredible arrangement to help their youngsters. They fantasize about offering their kids a preferred life over they had.

Discipline. Guardians know that restraining a youngster is difficult. Although it's seldom valued, it's not unexpected in the youngster's wellbeing.

Moral obligation. Guardians realize that it takes a town to bring up a youngster, yet they don't rethink liability regarding building a solid groundwork for their children. They likewise help their youngsters to acknowledge liability regarding their activities and decisions.

Compassion. Guardians instruct kids that achievement is the consequence of difficult work. What's more, albeit periodic disillusionment is unavoidable, they shouldn't allow it to crash the excursion. Guardians are dependably there to give a beam of daylight when the sky loads up with mists.

Inward voice. At the point when children grow up, they hear their parent's voices in their psyche. Ensure the words they hear offer positive messages.

Setting a model. Guardians realize their conduct will be imitated. Thusly, they can ingrain great individual qualities and a solid hard working attitude by filling in as excellent good examples.

Besides, they know that loved ones, instructors and ministers, VIPs and competitors, and even computer games, motion pictures, and music impact conduct. Might it be said that they are fortunate or unfortunate impacts?

Family. The family furnishes a kid with roots, genuinely necessary design, and unqualified love. Families likewise give their kids a cheerful home - - where a kid is generally protected and welcome.

While you're constructing another house, you first need to guarantee that you're introducing your home on substantial groundwork with the best soil conditions.

You then get to watch the various periods of your home as they are finished to make your last home. Very much like structure, another house requires areas of strength for an establishment to keep it immovably planted; youngsters additionally need serious areas of strength for an establishment as it is a crucial time in their lives.

Youth is when kids begin growing new abilities and interests and get to extend their wings. In this article, you will realize the reason why youth care and schooling, otherwise called ECCE is significant, and why you ought to seek after it for your little ones.

It's Not Just About Academics

Many individuals imagine that youth instruction is just about learning the letter set and numbers, notwithstanding, it's such a ton more extensive than that. Youngsters don't simply master essential abilities during that time; they get abilities including:

Interactive abilities: they get to play with different children and structure social connections

Profound abilities: they begin perceiving their sentiments and feelings, permitting them to impart and improve critical thinking abilities for what's in store

Mental abilities: they become presented to scholastics, and acquire phonological and mental abilities

Youngsters begin to collaborate with instructors and offspring of their age, creating abilities they could never have created had they remained at home as opposed to beginning their instructive excursion.

As per the United Nations, Educational, Scientific and Cultural Organization (UNESCO), youth instruction and care isn't just groundwork for grade school, yet rather a comprehensive improvement of a baby's mental, social, physical, and close-to-home requirements.

This comprehensive improvement targets constructing a strong starting point until the end of their lives, sustaining mindful, instructed, and caring future residents.

Building Trust

At the point when youngsters meet their instructors consistently, they begin to settle in and construct entrust with them. At the point when they begin believing individuals around them, this works with the educational experience and assists educators with enhancing nurturing endeavors, particularly if they're working guardians.

For that reason, educators should know every one of their understudies' advantages, cause them to feel quiet, offer them consideration, and empower them so they learn substantially more rapidly. Instructors can have a well-established effect on kids' lives, we as a whole most likely recall our kindergarten and grade teachers who gave us love and care.

Remember that an educator's job in early childcare isn't sufficient, guardians ought to remain involved too, and educators ought to work with them intently. Dr. Jessica Alvarado, a scholarly BA chief in Early Childhood Development at National University, expresses that when there's an organization among families and educators, this can extraordinarily impact the youngster's life and make the educational experience significantly more fruitful.

The Child's Brain

Youngsters' minds foster more than some other phases of their lives in the initial 5 years of their lives. Around 90% of mind development occurs before the age of 3, and afterward, it is completely developed when they're in kindergarten.

To that end, it is crucial to exploit this stage through youth care and education.

Children are subject to their family and first instructors during these long stretches of their lives to support them and assist them with fostering the right abilities and meeting the world.

Guardians can uphold sound mind development by giving youngsters a protected climate with plenty of chances to learn, investigate, and play. Youngsters learn best when their inclinations are evoked, which is the reason educators and experts show kids by presenting them with tunes, books, and stories that can foster their language abilities and assist them with acquiring information. So youth training can improve youngsters' mental health and set them up for school.

Discourse

Many guardians deal with issues when their youngsters aren't talking by the age of three. They then, at that point, begin taking them to subject matter experts, leaving them on a rollercoaster of language courses and long courses of anti-infection agents.

ECCE can assist guardians with keeping away from this issue, as youngsters will have a consciousness of their environmental factors almost immediately, the kid's jargon relies heavily on how frequently they speak with individuals, and how grown-ups converse with them.

Youngsters who don't get early training are tended to like infants until they have a school assessment nevertheless can't frame reasonable words or sentences.

Youth care and training is a difficult encounter for the two guardians and their youngsters. It's when kids leave their homes interestingly and begin gaining from individuals other than their folks.

Albeit testing, ECCE is of most extreme significance as it is the start of their instructive excursion, and will permit them to develop, create, and gain trust in their abilities and the individuals around them.

Chapter 4

The most effective method to support appropriate conduct in your youngster

Kids rapidly figure out how to act when they get positive, predictable directions from you. This implies offering your kid consideration when they act well, as opposed to simply applying outcomes when your kid accomplishes something you could do without.

Here are a few down-to-earth ways to set this positive methodology in motion.

Tips for a good way of behaving

1. Be a good example
Utilize your way of behaving to direct your youngster. Your kid watches you get pieces of information on the most proficient method to act - and what you do is in many cases considerably more significant than

what you say. For instance, assuming you believe that your kid should say 'kindly', say it yourself. If you don't believe your kid should speak loudly, talk unobtrusively and delicately yourself.

2. Show your kid how you feel
Telling your kid genuinely what their conduct means for you assist your kid with seeing their sentiments in yours. Also, assuming you start sentences with 'I', it allows your kid the opportunity to see things according to your viewpoint. For instance, 'I'm feeling upset since there's such an uproar and I can't chat on the telephone.

3. Discover your youngster being 'great'
At the point when your kid is acting in a manner you like, give your kid some sure criticism. For instance, 'Amazing, you're playing so pleasantly. I truly like how you're keeping every one of the blocks on the table. This works better compared to trusting that the blocks will come colliding with the floor

before you pay heed and say, 'Hello, stop that'.

This positive criticism is in some cases called elucidating acclaim since it tells kids explicitly the thing they're getting along nicely. Attempt to offer five positive remarks for each bad remark. What's more, recall that assuming that kids stand out or have negative considerations, they'll frequently search out bad considerations.

4. Get down to your youngster's level

At the point when you draw near to your kid, you can check out the thing they may be feeling or thinking. Being close additionally assists your kid with zeroing in on what you're talking about and their way of behaving. If you're near your kid and stand out enough to be noticed, you don't have to make them check you out.

5. Listen effectively

To listen effectively, you can gesture as your kid talks, and rehash back what you think your kid is feeling. For instance, 'It seems like you feel truly miserable that your blocks tumbled down. The point when you do this is it can assist small kids with adapting to pressure and large feelings like disappointment, which at times lead to undesirable ways of behaving. It additionally causes them to feel regarded and helped. It might diffuse potential hissy fits.

6. Keep guarantees

At the point when you keep your word, positive or negative, your kid figures out how to trust and regard you. Your kid discovers that you won't let them down when you've guaranteed something pleasant, and your kid likewise learns not to attempt to adjust your perspective when you've made sense of an outcome. So when you vow to take a stroll after your kid gets their toys, ensure you have your strolling shoes convenient. At the point when you say you'll leave the library if your kid doesn't quit going around, be ready to leave straight away.

7. Establish a climate for a good way of behaving

The climate around your kid can impact their way of behaving, so you can shape the climate to assist your kid with acting great. This can be as straightforward as ensuring your kid's space has a lot of protected, invigorating things for your youngster to play with. Likewise, ensure that your kid can't arrive at things they could break or that could hurt them.

8. Pick your fights

Before you engage in whatever your kid is doing - particularly to say 'no' or 'stop' - inquire as to whether it truly matters. By keeping directions, demands, and pessimistic input to a base, you set out fewer open doors for struggle and terrible sentiments. You can utilize family rules to tell everybody truly significant to your loved ones.

9. Be firm about crying
Assuming you give in when your kid is whimpering for something, you can coincidentally prepare your kid to cry more. 'No' signifies 'no', not 'perhaps', so don't say it except if you would not joke about this.

10. Keep things basic and positive
Guidelines ought to be clear, short, and fitting for your youngster's age, so your kid can comprehend and recollect them. What's more, positive principles are generally better compared to negative ones, since they positively guide your kid's conduct. For instance, 'If it's not too much trouble, shut the entryway' is better than 'Don't leave the door open'.

11. Give kids liability - and outcomes

As your kid ages, you can give your kid greater obligation regarding their way of behaving. You can likewise allow your kid the opportunity to encounter the normal results of that way of behaving. For instance, assuming it's your youngster's liability to pack for a sleepover and your kid fails to remember their #1 pad, the normal result is that your kid should oversee without the cushion for the evening.

At different times you could have to give outcomes to an improper or unsuitable way of behaving. For these times, ensure that you've made sense of the outcomes and your kid has consented to them ahead of time.

12. Let's assume it once and continue on

Assuming you instruct your kid - or what not to do - again and again, your kid could wind up blocking out. If you have any desire to allow your kid one final opportunity to collaborate, help your kid to remember the ramifications of not coordinating. Then, at that point, begin building up to three.

13. Allow your kid the opportunity to succeed

Put your youngster in a position to act well, and afterward acclaim them for it. For instance, give your youngster a few basic tasks or things that your kid can do to help the family. Commending your kid's way of behaving and exertion will urge your youngster to proceed. Furthermore, providing your kid with a great deal of work on doing an errand assists them with getting better at it, being happy-go-lucky about getting it done, and needing to continue to get it done.

14. Get ready for testing circumstances

There are times when addressing your kid's requirements and doing things you want to do will be precarious - for instance, while you're shopping, in the vehicle, or at an arrangement. Assuming that you ponder these difficult circumstances ahead of time, you can design around your kid's necessities. Give your kid a five-minute admonition before you want them to change exercises. Converse with your kid about why you want their participation. Then, at that point, your kid is ready for what you anticipate.

15. Keep a comical inclination

It frequently assists with keeping a day-to-day existence with youngsters light. You can do this by utilizing tunes, humor, and tomfoolery. For instance, you can claim to be the threatening stimulate beast who needs the toys lifted off the floor. Humor that has you both snickering is perfect, however, humor to your kid's detriment won't help. Small kids are effortlessly wounded by parental 'prodding'

Chapter 5

Having significant discussions with your children can be extreme. We've all inquired, "How was your day?" and got the feared single-word answers of "Good" and "Fine."

Here are a couple of tips to rouse great discussion and get your children to open up dependent upon you with more than those nonexclusive single-syllable answers.

Pose Open-Ended Inquiries

Rather than posing inquiries that can be addressed with only a single word, pose unassuming inquiries. Request kids what their number one sections from the day were or how they managed their dearest companions that day. At the point when they reply, proceed with the discussion with follow-up questions.

Eliminate Distractions

Carve out an opportunity to completely draw in with your kid during discussions and, in particular, pay attention to him. That implies switching off the TV, wireless, and tablets, and giving him full eye-to-eye connection. If the telephone rings, let it can hold on until after your discussion. Offering your kid your full consideration shows that you regard him and what he needs to say means quite a bit to you.

Practice It regularly

Take time consistently to discuss with your children. The hour of the day is different for everybody. For some's purposes, the superb open door is on the ride to and from school. Others chat best as a family during supper.

A few families even circumvent the table, every individual sharing the best and most exceedingly terrible piece of his day. This turns into a propensity and pushes the discussion along all through the whole dinner. I've seen my girl is normally eager to inform me regarding her school day on the ride home from school.

Be that as it may, at sleep time while we're cuddling, she opens up dependent upon me about more profound things she's been pondering day in and day out. That is the point at which we have the best discussions. Consider when your children feel the happiest with opening up dependent upon you.

Know What's Going On

My little girl's instructor sends a day-to-day email telling us what they discovered that day, as well as fun things that occurred. These messages are astonishing, and I focus on it to peruse the email before I get her from school.

I've understood on the off chance that I didn't find out about a portion of the fascinating things they did in the homeroom that day, that my little girl doesn't remember to refer to them to me more often than not.

Presently I can say, "Accomplished something exceptional occur at break today?" Usually, she will get energized and fill me in regarding what was unique that day. If your kid's educator doesn't send messages, take a stab at perusing school bulletins, getting some information about the day when you get your kid, or getting to know your youngsters' companions and their folks.

Get serious about Your Day

Discussions are a two-way road. At the point when you pose such a large number of inquiries, children might feel like they're being cross-examined. Open up and converse with them about your day. They love to hear what you did while they were in school.

Talk with your companion about his day before your youngsters as well. Displaying great correspondence with your companion will urge youngsters to jump into the discussion every day. Before your know it, your children will begin inquiring, "How was your day, Dad?" and "What did you do at work today, Mom?"

Hang out

Taking a walk, cooking together, or simply watching a film can assist with motivating discussion. While you're accomplishing something together, youngsters are substantially more prone to open up.

In a laid-back setting, they could begin a discussion with you that is considerably more significant to them than responding to the many inquiries you pose to them after school consistently. Once in a while telling children you're there to talk can be the best exhortation, and when they're agreeable, they will begin the discussion.

Evaluate these 20 ice breakers during supper:

Who is your closest companion and why?

What do you expect to do in 10 years?

What things are on your list of must-dos?

What is your number one method for investing your free energy and why?

If you could eat one nourishment until the end of your life, what might it be?

What is a truly amazing job?

What is your most humiliating second?

What qualities do you respect most in individuals you know?

What are the number one things we do all together?

How might you respond on the off chance that we could switch places for a day?

What are the most intriguing things about you?

What are you most pleased with in your life?

What is it that you need to be at the point at which you grow up and why?

If you had 1,000,000 bucks, how might you manage it?

What is your earliest memory?

What might your ideal day comprise?

If we could go anyplace with an extended get-away, where might you need to go?

What's your number one memory of us?

What is your greatest trepidation?

If you could eat with anybody, who might it, and could you discuss it?

Do you struggle with conversing with your children?

Novice guardians might track down this test because of language hindrances or squeezing settlement concerns. They can make some harder memories of interfacing with their children when their youngsters become better at communicating in English and begin holding with their colleagues.

Different guardians might be encountering society shock or battling with work and funds, making them less accessible to their children. What's more, assuming your kid is a juvenile, changes that accompany adolescence can additionally muddle what is happening.

Taking into account that rookie youngsters are likewise going through numerous changes, fabricating a cherishing and open relationship with your children is vital now. Your help is fundamental for their smooth incorporation and advancement into balanced grown-ups. Correspondence is a vital piece of this relationship.

Procedures to further develop correspondence:

Be accessible
Tell your kid that they can converse with you whenever. This can be hard thinking about your bustling life. Yet, recollect, you

moved to another nation so your kids can have a decent life, correct? Perhaps it is simply a question of rearranging your needs. Make the most of your discussions by truly tuning in. Remain mindful and intrigued by what your kid is talking about. Continuously guarantee them that you are prepared to comprehend and offer help.

Try not to pass judgment

Avoid rushing to make judgment calls and offer guidance immediately. Allow your kid to complete their story before you respond.

Most children don't converse with their folks since they're apprehensive about getting a negative response. They would rather not be reproved or accused. A few children likewise don't converse with their folks to try not to worry them.

They may not show it constantly but rather they know and value how hard their folks work and they would rather not add to their weight. So when they do converse with you, simply be open. Attempt and keep your tone nonpartisan when you talk. Comprehend what they need from you right now. Maybe all they need is so that you might be able to listen to them and that's it.

Get clarification on pressing issues

Before responding, pose inquiries smoothly. This will show that you are tuning in and need to know more. Attempt and pose unconditional inquiries (like by what means) to move the discussion along. Generally, you'll find what your kid truly needs to say through follow-up questions.

Utilize your local language

Your youngster won't find it harder to learn English on the off chance that they utilize your local language at home. There have been many investigations supporting bilingualism and its advantages to kids.

Guardians and teachers see that when the main language is deeply rooted, it assists the kid with learning the subsequent language better. One more obvious explanation: Since you can articulate your thoughts better in your local language, you might have the option to offer more help to your kids.

Make it a custom

Investigate them consistently. Exploit breakfast time, the vehicle ride to school, supper time, or before sleep time. Keep the discussion light.

Share your encounters with your children and urge them to do likewise. Showing a functioning interest in their exercises lets them know that you give it a second thought. This will assist them with turning out to be more open.

Be steady

Model open correspondence in the family with other relatives. Kids advance as a visual cue. If they see that they won't be mocked, disregarded, or messed with when they talk, they will be urged to open up. This is a cycle and may take some time. In any case, the more you make it happen, the simpler it will turn into.

Try not to allow contraptions to disrupt the general flow

Cell phones, tablets, game control centers, and even the TV can hamper certified correspondence. Limit device use during family time. First off, be a genuine model and be sans contraption when you're at home. You can look at your telephone later at night for any pressing messages.

Look into their inclinations

One of the most incredible ways of having a significant discussion with your children is to have a shared view. Why not share their advantage in a game or side interest?

Or on the other hand maybe watch a film or a TV series that they like? This will open up countless subjects to discuss with your kids. It's an incredible method for investing energy and bonding with them.

www.ingramcontent.com/pod-product-compliance
Lightning Source LLC
LaVergne TN
LVHW052055160826
845678LV00015B/3234

* 9 7 9 8 8 4 8 5 8 5 5 5 1 *